THIS BOOK BELONGS TO:
_____
_____
_____

TABLE OF CONTENTS:

WISH LIST PAGE 7
GARDEN BUDGET PAGE 11
SEED INVENTORY PAGE 13
GARDEN LAYOUT PLANNER PAGE 19
SEED STARTING SCHEDULE PAGE 43
SOIL AMENDMENT AND FERTILIZER TRACKER PAGE 49
BLANK CALENDAR PAGE 55
SPRING CHORES AND PROJECTS PAGE 79
SUMMER CHORES AND PROJECTS PAGE 81
FALL CHORES AND PROJECTS PAGE 83
WINTER CHORES AND PROJECTS PAGE 85
GARDEN TOUR 89
PROBLEMS AND PESTS PAGE 101
PLANT PROFILE PAGE 107
NEXT YEARS WISH LIST PAGE 179
YEAR END NOTES PAGE 189

USE THE FOLLOWING PAGES TO PLAN YOUR WIST LIST
AND BUDGET FOR THE SEASON.
INVENTORY YOUR SEEDS, PLAN FOR NEW SEEDS,
PLANTS, LANDSCAPING, ETC

YOUR WISH LIST IS A PLACE TO DREAM ABOUT THE SEASON TO COME

WISH LIST

ITEM

WISH LIST

ITEM

WISH LIST

ITEM

WISH LIST

ITEM

GARDEN BUDGET

ITEM	PROJECTED COST	ACTUAL COST
TOTAL		

GARDEN BUDGET

ITEM	PROJECTED COST	ACTUAL COST
TOTAL		

SEED INVENTORY

SEED	VARIETY	QTY	PURCHASE DATE	SEED COMPANY	GROW AGAIN?

SEED INVENTORY

SEED	VARIETY	QTY	PURCHASE DATE	SEED COMPANY	GROW AGAIN?

SEED INVENTORY

SEED	VARIETY	QTY	PURCHASE DATE	SEED COMPANY	GROW AGAIN?

SEED INVENTORY

SEED	VARIETY	QTY	PURCHASE DATE	SEED COMPANY	GROW AGAIN?

USE THE FOLLOWING PAGES
TO PLAN YOUR GARDEN LAYOUT,
WHEN TO START YOUR SEEDS
AND WHAT AMENDMENTS ARE
NEEDED FOR THE GROWING SEASON.

THIS IS WHERE YOUR DREAMS START
TO BECOME A GROWING REALITY

GARDEN LAYOUT PLANNER
USE THE SQUARES TO PLAN YOUR LAYOUT
AND THE LINED SECTION TO WRITE NOTES

GARDEN LAYOUT PLANNER
USE THE SQUARES TO PLAN YOUR LAYOUT
AND THE LINED SECTION TO WRITE NOTES

GARDEN LAYOUT PLANNER
USE THE SQUARES TO PLAN YOUR LAYOUT
AND THE LINED SECTION TO WRITE NOTES

GARDEN LAYOUT PLANNER
USE THE SQUARES TO PLAN YOUR LAYOUT AND THE LINED SECTION TO WRITE NOTES

GARDEN LAYOUT PLANNER
USE THE SQUARES TO PLAN YOUR LAYOUT
AND THE LINED SECTION TO WRITE NOTES

GARDEN LAYOUT PLANNER
USE THE SQUARES TO PLAN YOUR LAYOUT
AND THE LINED SECTION TO WRITE NOTES

GARDEN LAYOUT PLANNER
USE THE SQUARES TO PLAN YOUR LAYOUT
AND THE LINED SECTION TO WRITE NOTES

GARDEN LAYOUT PLANNER
USE THE SQUARES TO PLAN YOUR LAYOUT
AND THE LINED SECTION TO WRITE NOTES

GARDEN LAYOUT PLANNER
USE THE SQUARES TO PLAN YOUR LAYOUT
AND THE LINED SECTION TO WRITE NOTES

GARDEN LAYOUT PLANNER
USE THE SQUARES TO PLAN YOUR LAYOUT
AND THE LINED SECTION TO WRITE NOTES

GARDEN LAYOUT PLANNER
USE THE SQUARES TO PLAN YOUR LAYOUT AND THE LINED SECTION TO WRITE NOTES

GARDEN LAYOUT PLANNER
USE THE SQUARES TO PLAN YOUR LAYOUT
AND THE LINED SECTION TO WRITE NOTES

GARDEN LAYOUT PLANNER
USE THE SQUARES TO PLAN YOUR LAYOUT AND THE LINED SECTION TO WRITE NOTES

GARDEN LAYOUT PLANNER
USE THE SQUARES TO PLAN YOUR LAYOUT AND THE LINED SECTION TO WRITE NOTES

GARDEN LAYOUT PLANNER
USE THE SQUARES TO PLAN YOUR LAYOUT
AND THE LINED SECTION TO WRITE NOTES

GARDEN LAYOUT PLANNER
USE THE SQUARES TO PLAN YOUR LAYOUT
AND THE LINED SECTION TO WRITE NOTES

GARDEN LAYOUT PLANNER
USE THE SQUARES TO PLAN YOUR LAYOUT
AND THE LINED SECTION TO WRITE NOTES

GARDEN LAYOUT PLANNER
USE THE SQUARES TO PLAN YOUR LAYOUT
AND THE LINED SECTION TO WRITE NOTES

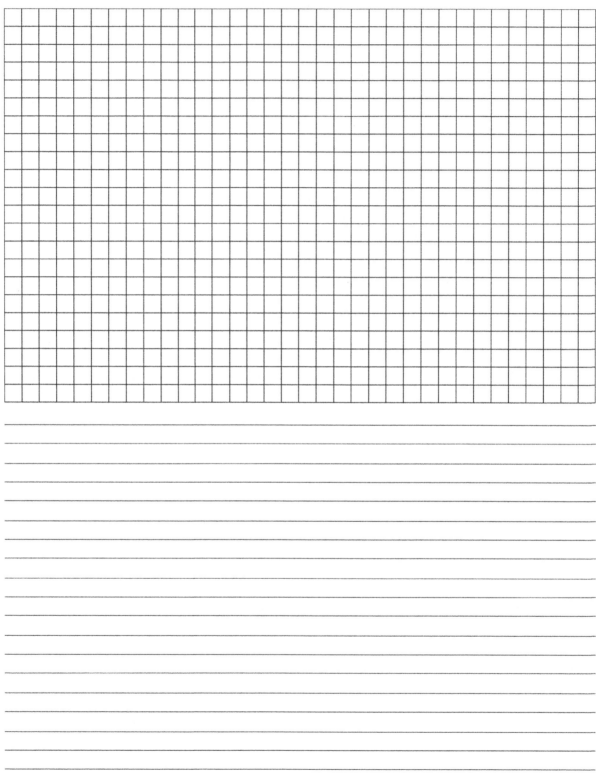

GARDEN LAYOUT PLANNER
USE THE SQUARES TO PLAN YOUR LAYOUT
AND THE LINED SECTION TO WRITE NOTES

GARDEN LAYOUT PLANNER
USE THE SQUARES TO PLAN YOUR LAYOUT AND THE LINED SECTION TO WRITE NOTES

GARDEN LAYOUT PLANNER
USE THE SQUARES TO PLAN YOUR LAYOUT AND THE LINED SECTION TO WRITE NOTES

GARDEN LAYOUT PLANNER
USE THE SQUARES TO PLAN YOUR LAYOUT
AND THE LINED SECTION TO WRITE NOTES

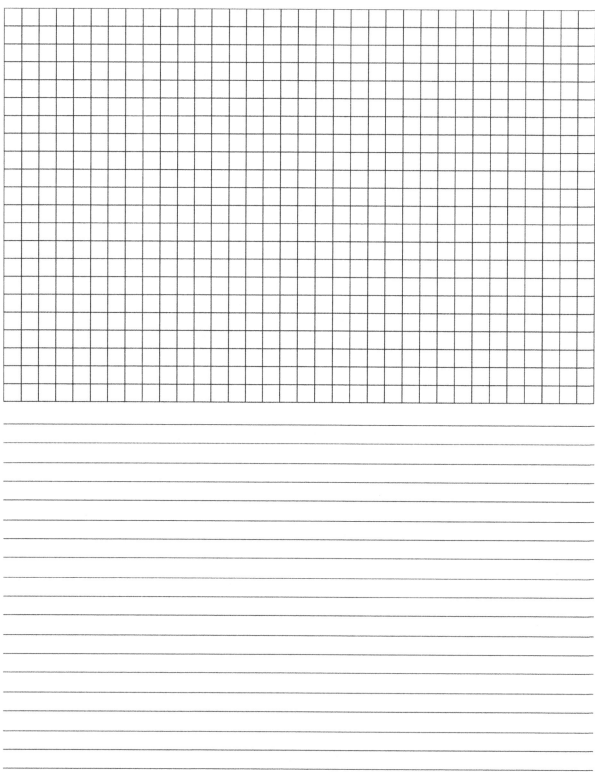

GARDEN LAYOUT PLANNER
USE THE SQUARES TO PLAN YOUR LAYOUT
AND THE LINED SECTION TO WRITE NOTES

GARDEN LAYOUT PLANNER
USE THE SQUARES TO PLAN YOUR LAYOUT
AND THE LINED SECTION TO WRITE NOTES

SEED STARTING SCHEDULE

SEED	DATE SOWN	TRANSPLANT DATE	BLOOM AND OR HARVEST DATE	NOTES

SEED STARTING SCHEDULE

SEED	DATE SOWN	TRANSPLANT DATE	BLOOM AND OR HARVEST DATE	NOTES

SEED STARTING SCHEDULE

SEED	DATE SOWN	TRANSPLANT DATE	BLOOM AND OR HARVEST DATE	NOTES

SEED STARTING SCHEDULE

SEED	DATE SOWN	TRANSPLANT DATE	BLOOM AND OR HARVEST DATE	NOTES

SEED STARTING SCHEDULE

SEED	DATE SOWN	TRANSPLANT DATE	BLOOM AND OR HARVEST DATE	NOTES

SEED STARTING SCHEDULE

SEED	DATE SOWN	TRANSPLANT DATE	BLOOM AND OR HARVEST DATE	NOTES

SOIL AMENDMENT AND FERTILIZER TRACKER

AMENDMENT	DATE	RESULT

SOIL AMENDMENT AND FERTILIZER TRACKER

AMENDMENT	DATE	RESULT

SOIL AMENDMENT AND FERTILIZER TRACKER

AMENDMENT	DATE	RESULT

SOIL AMENDMENT AND FERTILIZER TRACKER

AMENDMENT	DATE	RESULT

USE THE FOLLOWING BLANK CALENDAR PAGES AND SEASON BY SEASON CHORES AND PROJECTS PAGES TO KEEP YOU ON TRACK THROUGHOUT THE YEAR

STAYING ORGANIZED CAN HELP YOU TO HAVE A BOUNTIFUL HARVEST

MONTH ☐   YEAR ☐

FILL IN EACH SPACE WITH THE DATE AND ACTIVITY

MONTH ☐ YEAR ☐

FILL IN EACH SPACE WITH THE DATE AND ACTIVITY

MONTH ☐   YEAR ☐

FILL IN EACH SPACE WITH THE DATE AND ACTIVITY

MONTH ☐   YEAR ☐

FILL IN EACH SPACE WITH THE DATE AND ACTIVITY

MONTH ☐ YEAR ☐

FILL IN EACH SPACE WITH THE DATE AND ACTIVITY

MONTH ☐   YEAR ☐

FILL IN EACH SPACE WITH THE DATE AND ACTIVITY

MONTH ☐ YEAR ☐

FILL IN EACH SPACE WITH THE DATE AND ACTIVITY

MONTH ☐   YEAR ☐

FILL IN EACH SPACE WITH THE DATE AND ACTIVITY

MONTH ☐ YEAR ☐

FILL IN EACH SPACE WITH THE DATE AND ACTIVITY

MONTH ☐   YEAR ☐

FILL IN EACH SPACE WITH THE DATE AND ACTIVITY

MONTH ☐   YEAR ☐

FILL IN EACH SPACE WITH THE DATE AND ACTIVITY

MONTH [ ] YEAR [ ]

FILL IN EACH SPACE WITH THE DATE AND ACTIVITY

SPRING CHORES AND PROJECTS

DATE STARTED	PROJECT	DATE COMPLETED

SPRING CHORES AND PROJECTS

DATE STARTED	PROJECT	DATE COMPLETED

SUMMER CHORES AND PROJECTS

DATE STARTED	PROJECT	DATE COMPLETED

SUMMER CHORES AND PROJECTS

DATE STARTED	PROJECT	DATE COMPLETED

FALL CHORES AND PROJECTS

DATE STARTED	PROJECT	DATE COMPLETED

FALL CHORES AND PROJECTS

DATE STARTED	PROJECT	DATE COMPLETED

WINTER CHORES AND PROJECTS

DATE STARTED	PROJECT	DATE COMPLETED

WINTER CHORES AND PROJECTS

DATE STARTED	PROJECT	DATE COMPLETED

USE THE FOLLOWING PAGES TO REGULARY
TRACK YOUR GARDEN.
TOURING YOUR GARDEN ON A REGULAR
BASIS WILL HELP YOU
TO FIND ANY PESTS OR PROBLEMS EARLY ON

PESTS DO NOT STAND A CHANCE WITH YOU ON THE LOOKOUT

GARDEN TOUR

TOUR YOUR GARDEN REGULARLY TO STAY ON TOP OF PESTS AND PROBLEMS

DATE _____

TASKS _____

WEATHER NOTES _____

WHATS GROWING _____

HARVEST _____

PESTS AND PROBLEMS _____

DATE _____

TASKS _____

WEATHER NOTES _____

WHATS GROWING _____

HARVEST _____

PESTS AND PROBLEMS _____

DATE _____

TASKS _____

WEATHER NOTES _____

WHATS GROWING _____

HARVEST _____

PESTS AND PROBLEMS _____

DATE _____

TASKS _____

WEATHER NOTES _____

WHATS GROWING _____

HARVEST _____

PESTS AND PROBLEMS _____

GARDEN TOUR

TOUR YOUR GARDEN REGULARLY TO STAY ON TOP OF PESTS AND PROBLEMS

DATE _____

TASKS _____

WEATHER NOTES _____

WHATS GROWING _____

HARVEST _____

PESTS AND PROBLEMS _____

DATE _____

TASKS _____

WEATHER NOTES _____

WHATS GROWING _____

HARVEST _____

PESTS AND PROBLEMS _____

DATE _____

TASKS _____

WEATHER NOTES _____

WHATS GROWING _____

HARVEST _____

PESTS AND PROBLEMS _____

DATE _____

TASKS _____

WEATHER NOTES _____

WHATS GROWING _____

HARVEST _____

PESTS AND PROBLEMS _____

GARDEN TOUR
TOUR YOUR GARDEN REGULARLY TO STAY ON TOP OF PESTS AND PROBLEMS

DATE _____

TASKS _____

WEATHER NOTES _____

WHATS GROWING _____

HARVEST _____

PESTS AND PROBLEMS _____

DATE _____

TASKS _____

WEATHER NOTES _____

WHATS GROWING _____

HARVEST _____

PESTS AND PROBLEMS _____

DATE _____

TASKS _____

WEATHER NOTES _____

WHATS GROWING _____

HARVEST _____

PESTS AND PROBLEMS _____

DATE _____

TASKS _____

WEATHER NOTES _____

WHATS GROWING _____

HARVEST _____

PESTS AND PROBLEMS _____

GARDEN TOUR
TOUR YOUR GARDEN REGULARLY TO STAY ON TOP OF PESTS AND PROBLEMS

DATE _____

TASKS _____

WEATHER NOTES _____

WHATS GROWING _____

HARVEST _____

PESTS AND PROBLEMS _____

DATE _____

TASKS _____

WEATHER NOTES _____

WHATS GROWING _____

HARVEST _____

PESTS AND PROBLEMS _____

DATE _____

TASKS _____

WEATHER NOTES _____

WHATS GROWING _____

HARVEST _____

PESTS AND PROBLEMS _____

DATE _____

TASKS _____

WEATHER NOTES _____

WHATS GROWING _____

HARVEST _____

PESTS AND PROBLEMS _____

GARDEN TOUR

TOUR YOUR GARDEN REGULARLY TO STAY ON TOP OF PESTS AND PROBLEMS

DATE _____
TASKS _____
WEATHER NOTES _____
WHATS GROWING _____
HARVEST _____
PESTS AND PROBLEMS _____

DATE _____
TASKS _____
WEATHER NOTES _____
WHATS GROWING _____
HARVEST _____
PESTS AND PROBLEMS _____

DATE _____
TASKS _____
WEATHER NOTES _____
WHATS GROWING _____
HARVEST _____
PESTS AND PROBLEMS _____

DATE _____
TASKS _____
WEATHER NOTES _____
WHATS GROWING _____
HARVEST _____
PESTS AND PROBLEMS _____

GARDEN TOUR

TOUR YOUR GARDEN REGULARLY TO STAY ON TOP OF PESTS AND PROBLEMS

DATE _____

TASKS _____

WEATHER NOTES _____

WHATS GROWING _____

HARVEST _____

PESTS AND PROBLEMS _____

DATE _____

TASKS _____

WEATHER NOTES _____

WHATS GROWING _____

HARVEST _____

PESTS AND PROBLEMS _____

DATE _____

TASKS _____

WEATHER NOTES _____

WHATS GROWING _____

HARVEST _____

PESTS AND PROBLEMS _____

DATE _____

TASKS _____

WEATHER NOTES _____

WHATS GROWING _____

HARVEST _____

PESTS AND PROBLEMS _____

GARDEN TOUR

TOUR YOUR GARDEN REGULARLY TO STAY ON TOP OF PESTS AND PROBLEMS

DATE _____

TASKS _____

WEATHER NOTES _____

WHATS GROWING _____

HARVEST _____

PESTS AND PROBLEMS _____

DATE _____

TASKS _____

WEATHER NOTES _____

WHATS GROWING _____

HARVEST _____

PESTS AND PROBLEMS _____

DATE _____

TASKS _____

WEATHER NOTES _____

WHATS GROWING _____

HARVEST _____

PESTS AND PROBLEMS _____

DATE _____

TASKS _____

WEATHER NOTES _____

WHATS GROWING _____

HARVEST _____

PESTS AND PROBLEMS _____

GARDEN TOUR
TOUR YOUR GARDEN REGULARLY TO STAY ON TOP OF PESTS AND PROBLEMS

DATE _____

TASKS _____

WEATHER NOTES _____

WHATS GROWING _____

HARVEST _____

PESTS AND PROBLEMS _____

DATE _____

TASKS _____

WEATHER NOTES _____

WHATS GROWING _____

HARVEST _____

PESTS AND PROBLEMS _____

DATE _____

TASKS _____

WEATHER NOTES _____

WHATS GROWING _____

HARVEST _____

PESTS AND PROBLEMS _____

DATE _____

TASKS _____

WEATHER NOTES _____

WHATS GROWING _____

HARVEST _____

PESTS AND PROBLEMS _____

GARDEN TOUR

TOUR YOUR GARDEN REGULARLY TO STAY ON TOP OF PESTS AND PROBLEMS

DATE _____

TASKS _____

WEATHER NOTES _____

WHATS GROWING _____

HARVEST _____

PESTS AND PROBLEMS _____

DATE _____

TASKS _____

WEATHER NOTES _____

WHATS GROWING _____

HARVEST _____

PESTS AND PROBLEMS _____

DATE _____

TASKS _____

WEATHER NOTES _____

WHATS GROWING _____

HARVEST _____

PESTS AND PROBLEMS _____

DATE _____

TASKS _____

WEATHER NOTES _____

WHATS GROWING _____

HARVEST _____

PESTS AND PROBLEMS _____

GARDEN TOUR

TOUR YOUR GARDEN REGULARLY TO STAY ON TOP OF PESTS AND PROBLEMS

DATE _____

TASKS _____

WEATHER NOTES _____

WHATS GROWING _____

HARVEST _____

PESTS AND PROBLEMS _____

DATE _____

TASKS _____

WEATHER NOTES _____

WHATS GROWING _____

HARVEST _____

PESTS AND PROBLEMS _____

DATE _____

TASKS _____

WEATHER NOTES _____

WHATS GROWING _____

HARVEST _____

PESTS AND PROBLEMS _____

DATE _____

TASKS _____

WEATHER NOTES _____

WHATS GROWING _____

HARVEST _____

PESTS AND PROBLEMS _____

GARDEN TOUR
TOUR YOUR GARDEN REGULARLY TO STAY ON TOP OF PESTS AND PROBLEMS

DATE _____
TASKS _____
WEATHER NOTES _____
WHATS GROWING _____
HARVEST _____
PESTS AND PROBLEMS _____

DATE _____
TASKS _____
WEATHER NOTES _____
WHATS GROWING _____
HARVEST _____
PESTS AND PROBLEMS _____

DATE _____
TASKS _____
WEATHER NOTES _____
WHATS GROWING _____
HARVEST _____
PESTS AND PROBLEMS _____

DATE _____
TASKS _____
WEATHER NOTES _____
WHATS GROWING _____
HARVEST _____
PESTS AND PROBLEMS _____

GARDEN TOUR
TOUR YOUR GARDEN REGULARLY TO STAY ON TOP OF PESTS AND PROBLEMS

DATE _____

TASKS _____

WEATHER NOTES _____

WHATS GROWING _____

HARVEST _____

PESTS AND PROBLEMS _____

———————————————————

DATE _____

TASKS _____

WEATHER NOTES _____

WHATS GROWING _____

HARVEST _____

PESTS AND PROBLEMS _____

———————————————————

DATE _____

TASKS _____

WEATHER NOTES _____

WHATS GROWING _____

HARVEST _____

PESTS AND PROBLEMS _____

———————————————————

DATE _____

TASKS _____

WEATHER NOTES _____

WHATS GROWING _____

HARVEST _____

PESTS AND PROBLEMS _____

PROBLEMS AND PESTS

DATE	SOLUTION	EFFECTIVE Y/N

PROBLEMS AND PESTS

DATE	SOLUTION	EFFECTIVE Y/N

PROBLEMS AND PESTS

DATE	SOLUTION	EFFECTIVE Y/N

PROBLEMS AND PESTS

DATE	SOLUTION	EFFECTIVE Y/N

USE THE FOLLOWING PAGES TO RECORD ALL THE DETAILS ABOUT EACH PLANT YOU PLAN ON GROWING AND HOW TO CARE FOR IT

EVERY PLANT COMES WITH ITS OWN UNIQUE NEEDS

PLANT PROFILE

COMMON NAME _____

BOTANICAL NAME _____

DATE PLANTED _____ PURCHASED AT _____

LIGHT NEEDS _____ WATER NEEDS _____

SEED ☐   TRANSPLANT ☐

GROW AGAIN?   YES ☐   NO ☐

DATE	NOTES

PLANT PROFILE

COMMON NAME _____

BOTANICAL NAME _____

DATE PLANTED _____ PURCHASED AT _____

LIGHT NEEDS _____ WATER NEEDS _____

SEED ☐   TRANSPLANT ☐

GROW AGAIN?   YES ☐   NO ☐

DATE	NOTES

PLANT PROFILE

COMMON NAME _____

BOTANICAL NAME _____

DATE PLANTED _____ PURCHASED AT _____

LIGHT NEEDS _____ WATER NEEDS _____

SEED ☐   TRANSPLANT ☐

GROW AGAIN?   YES ☐   NO ☐

DATE	NOTES

PLANT PROFILE

COMMON NAME _____

BOTANICAL NAME _____

DATE PLANTED _____ PURCHASED AT _____

LIGHT NEEDS _____ WATER NEEDS _____

SEED ☐   TRANSPLANT ☐

GROW AGAIN?   YES ☐   NO ☐

DATE	NOTES

PLANT PROFILE

COMMON NAME _____

BOTANICAL NAME _____

DATE PLANTED _____ PURCHASED AT _____

LIGHT NEEDS _____ WATER NEEDS _____

SEED ☐   TRANSPLANT ☐

GROW AGAIN?   YES ☐   NO ☐

DATE	NOTES

PLANT PROFILE

COMMON NAME _____

BOTANICAL NAME _____

DATE PLANTED _____ PURCHASED AT _____

LIGHT NEEDS _____ WATER NEEDS _____

SEED ☐   TRANSPLANT ☐

GROW AGAIN?   YES ☐   NO ☐

DATE	NOTES

PLANT PROFILE

COMMON NAME _____

BOTANICAL NAME _____

DATE PLANTED _____ PURCHASED AT _____

LIGHT NEEDS _____ WATER NEEDS _____

SEED ☐   TRANSPLANT ☐

GROW AGAIN?   YES ☐   NO ☐

DATE	NOTES

PLANT PROFILE

COMMON NAME _____

BOTANICAL NAME _____

DATE PLANTED _____ PURCHASED AT _____

LIGHT NEEDS _____ WATER NEEDS _____

SEED ☐   TRANSPLANT ☐

GROW AGAIN?   YES ☐   NO ☐

DATE	NOTES

PLANT PROFILE

COMMON NAME _____

BOTANICAL NAME _____

DATE PLANTED _____ PURCHASED AT _____

LIGHT NEEDS _____ WATER NEEDS _____

SEED ☐   TRANSPLANT ☐

GROW AGAIN?   YES ☐   NO ☐

DATE	NOTES

PLANT PROFILE

COMMON NAME _____

BOTANICAL NAME _____

DATE PLANTED _____ PURCHASED AT _____

LIGHT NEEDS _____ WATER NEEDS _____

SEED ☐   TRANSPLANT ☐

GROW AGAIN?   YES ☐   NO ☐

DATE	NOTES

PLANT PROFILE

COMMON NAME _____

BOTANICAL NAME _____

DATE PLANTED _____ PURCHASED AT _____

LIGHT NEEDS _____ WATER NEEDS _____

SEED ☐   TRANSPLANT ☐

GROW AGAIN?   YES ☐   NO ☐

DATE	NOTES

PLANT PROFILE

COMMON NAME _____

BOTANICAL NAME _____

DATE PLANTED _____ PURCHASED AT _____

LIGHT NEEDS _____ WATER NEEDS _____

SEED ☐   TRANSPLANT ☐

GROW AGAIN?   YES ☐   NO ☐

DATE	NOTES

PLANT PROFILE

COMMON NAME _____

BOTANICAL NAME _____

DATE PLANTED _____ PURCHASED AT _____

LIGHT NEEDS _____ WATER NEEDS _____

SEED ☐   TRANSPLANT ☐

GROW AGAIN?   YES ☐   NO ☐

DATE	NOTES

PLANT PROFILE

COMMON NAME _____

BOTANICAL NAME _____

DATE PLANTED _____ PURCHASED AT _____

LIGHT NEEDS _____ WATER NEEDS _____

SEED ☐   TRANSPLANT ☐

GROW AGAIN?   YES ☐   NO ☐

DATE	NOTES

PLANT PROFILE

COMMON NAME _____

BOTANICAL NAME _____

DATE PLANTED _____ PURCHASED AT _____

LIGHT NEEDS _____ WATER NEEDS _____

SEED ☐   TRANSPLANT ☐

GROW AGAIN?   YES ☐   NO ☐

DATE	NOTES

PLANT PROFILE

COMMON NAME _____

BOTANICAL NAME _____

DATE PLANTED _____ PURCHASED AT _____

LIGHT NEEDS _____ WATER NEEDS _____

SEED ☐   TRANSPLANT ☐

GROW AGAIN?   YES ☐   NO ☐

DATE	NOTES

PLANT PROFILE

COMMON NAME _____

BOTANICAL NAME _____

DATE PLANTED _____ PURCHASED AT _____

LIGHT NEEDS _____ WATER NEEDS _____

SEED ☐   TRANSPLANT ☐

GROW AGAIN?   YES ☐   NO ☐

DATE	NOTES

PLANT PROFILE

COMMON NAME _____

BOTANICAL NAME _____

DATE PLANTED _____ PURCHASED AT _____

LIGHT NEEDS _____ WATER NEEDS _____

SEED ☐   TRANSPLANT ☐

GROW AGAIN?   YES ☐   NO ☐

DATE	NOTES

PLANT PROFILE

COMMON NAME _____

BOTANICAL NAME _____

DATE PLANTED _____ PURCHASED AT _____

LIGHT NEEDS _____ WATER NEEDS _____

SEED ☐   TRANSPLANT ☐

GROW AGAIN?   YES ☐   NO ☐

DATE	NOTES

PLANT PROFILE

COMMON NAME _____

BOTANICAL NAME _____

DATE PLANTED _____ PURCHASED AT _____

LIGHT NEEDS _____ WATER NEEDS _____

SEED ☐   TRANSPLANT ☐

GROW AGAIN?   YES ☐   NO ☐

DATE	NOTES

PLANT PROFILE

COMMON NAME _____

BOTANICAL NAME _____

DATE PLANTED _____ PURCHASED AT _____

LIGHT NEEDS _____ WATER NEEDS _____

SEED ☐   TRANSPLANT ☐

GROW AGAIN?   YES ☐   NO ☐

DATE	NOTES

PLANT PROFILE

COMMON NAME _____

BOTANICAL NAME _____

DATE PLANTED _____ PURCHASED AT _____

LIGHT NEEDS _____ WATER NEEDS _____

SEED ☐   TRANSPLANT ☐

GROW AGAIN?   YES ☐   NO ☐

DATE	NOTES

PLANT PROFILE

COMMON NAME _____

BOTANICAL NAME _____

DATE PLANTED _____ PURCHASED AT _____

LIGHT NEEDS _____ WATER NEEDS _____

SEED ☐   TRANSPLANT ☐

GROW AGAIN?   YES ☐   NO ☐

DATE	NOTES

PLANT PROFILE

COMMON NAME _____

BOTANICAL NAME _____

DATE PLANTED _____ PURCHASED AT _____

LIGHT NEEDS _____ WATER NEEDS _____

SEED ☐   TRANSPLANT ☐

GROW AGAIN?   YES ☐   NO ☐

DATE	NOTES

PLANT PROFILE

COMMON NAME _____

BOTANICAL NAME _____

DATE PLANTED _____ PURCHASED AT _____

LIGHT NEEDS _____ WATER NEEDS _____

SEED ☐   TRANSPLANT ☐

GROW AGAIN?   YES ☐   NO ☐

DATE	NOTES

PLANT PROFILE

COMMON NAME _____

BOTANICAL NAME _____

DATE PLANTED _____ PURCHASED AT _____

LIGHT NEEDS _____ WATER NEEDS _____

SEED ☐   TRANSPLANT ☐

GROW AGAIN?   YES ☐   NO ☐

DATE	NOTES

PLANT PROFILE

COMMON NAME _____

BOTANICAL NAME _____

DATE PLANTED _____ PURCHASED AT _____

LIGHT NEEDS _____ WATER NEEDS _____

SEED ☐   TRANSPLANT ☐

GROW AGAIN?   YES ☐   NO ☐

DATE	NOTES

PLANT PROFILE

COMMON NAME _____

BOTANICAL NAME _____

DATE PLANTED _____ PURCHASED AT _____

LIGHT NEEDS _____ WATER NEEDS _____

SEED ☐   TRANSPLANT ☐

GROW AGAIN?   YES ☐   NO ☐

DATE	NOTES

PLANT PROFILE

COMMON NAME _____

BOTANICAL NAME _____

DATE PLANTED _____ PURCHASED AT _____

LIGHT NEEDS _____ WATER NEEDS _____

SEED ☐   TRANSPLANT ☐

GROW AGAIN?   YES ☐   NO ☐

DATE	NOTES

PLANT PROFILE

COMMON NAME _____

BOTANICAL NAME _____

DATE PLANTED _____ PURCHASED AT _____

LIGHT NEEDS _____ WATER NEEDS _____

SEED ☐   TRANSPLANT ☐

GROW AGAIN?   YES ☐   NO ☐

DATE	NOTES

PLANT PROFILE

COMMON NAME _____

BOTANICAL NAME _____

DATE PLANTED _____ PURCHASED AT _____

LIGHT NEEDS _____ WATER NEEDS _____

SEED ☐   TRANSPLANT ☐

GROW AGAIN?   YES ☐   NO ☐

DATE	NOTES

PLANT PROFILE

COMMON NAME _____

BOTANICAL NAME _____

DATE PLANTED _____ PURCHASED AT _____

LIGHT NEEDS _____ WATER NEEDS _____

SEED ☐   TRANSPLANT ☐

GROW AGAIN?   YES ☐   NO ☐

DATE	NOTES

PLANT PROFILE

COMMON NAME _____

BOTANICAL NAME _____

DATE PLANTED _____ PURCHASED AT _____

LIGHT NEEDS _____ WATER NEEDS _____

SEED ☐   TRANSPLANT ☐

GROW AGAIN?   YES ☐   NO ☐

DATE	NOTES

PLANT PROFILE

COMMON NAME _____

BOTANICAL NAME _____

DATE PLANTED _____ PURCHASED AT _____

LIGHT NEEDS _____ WATER NEEDS _____

SEED ☐   TRANSPLANT ☐

GROW AGAIN?   YES ☐   NO ☐

DATE	NOTES

PLANT PROFILE

COMMON NAME _____

BOTANICAL NAME _____

DATE PLANTED _____ PURCHASED AT _____

LIGHT NEEDS _____ WATER NEEDS _____

SEED ☐   TRANSPLANT ☐

GROW AGAIN?   YES ☐   NO ☐

DATE	NOTES

PLANT PROFILE

COMMON NAME _____

BOTANICAL NAME _____

DATE PLANTED _____ PURCHASED AT _____

LIGHT NEEDS _____ WATER NEEDS _____

SEED ☐   TRANSPLANT ☐

GROW AGAIN?   YES ☐   NO ☐

DATE	NOTES

PLANT PROFILE

COMMON NAME _____

BOTANICAL NAME _____

DATE PLANTED _____ PURCHASED AT _____

LIGHT NEEDS _____ WATER NEEDS _____

SEED ☐   TRANSPLANT ☐

GROW AGAIN?   YES ☐   NO ☐

DATE	NOTES

PLANT PROFILE

COMMON NAME _____

BOTANICAL NAME _____

DATE PLANTED _____ PURCHASED AT _____

LIGHT NEEDS _____ WATER NEEDS _____

SEED ☐   TRANSPLANT ☐

GROW AGAIN?   YES ☐   NO ☐

DATE	NOTES

PLANT PROFILE

COMMON NAME _____

BOTANICAL NAME _____

DATE PLANTED _____ PURCHASED AT _____

LIGHT NEEDS _____ WATER NEEDS _____

SEED ☐   TRANSPLANT ☐

GROW AGAIN?   YES ☐   NO ☐

DATE	NOTES

PLANT PROFILE

COMMON NAME _____

BOTANICAL NAME _____

DATE PLANTED _____ PURCHASED AT _____

LIGHT NEEDS _____ WATER NEEDS _____

SEED ☐   TRANSPLANT ☐

GROW AGAIN?   YES ☐   NO ☐

DATE	NOTES

PLANT PROFILE

COMMON NAME _____

BOTANICAL NAME _____

DATE PLANTED _____ PURCHASED AT _____

LIGHT NEEDS _____ WATER NEEDS _____

SEED ☐   TRANSPLANT ☐

GROW AGAIN?   YES ☐   NO ☐

DATE	NOTES

PLANT PROFILE

COMMON NAME _____

BOTANICAL NAME _____

DATE PLANTED _____ PURCHASED AT _____

LIGHT NEEDS _____ WATER NEEDS _____

SEED ☐   TRANSPLANT ☐

GROW AGAIN?   YES ☐   NO ☐

DATE	NOTES

PLANT PROFILE

COMMON NAME _____

BOTANICAL NAME _____

DATE PLANTED _____ PURCHASED AT _____

LIGHT NEEDS _____ WATER NEEDS _____

SEED ☐   TRANSPLANT ☐

GROW AGAIN?   YES ☐   NO ☐

DATE	NOTES

PLANT PROFILE

COMMON NAME _____

BOTANICAL NAME _____

DATE PLANTED _____ PURCHASED AT _____

LIGHT NEEDS _____ WATER NEEDS _____

SEED ☐   TRANSPLANT ☐

GROW AGAIN?   YES ☐   NO ☐

DATE	NOTES

PLANT PROFILE

COMMON NAME _____

BOTANICAL NAME _____

DATE PLANTED _____ PURCHASED AT _____

LIGHT NEEDS _____ WATER NEEDS _____

SEED ☐   TRANSPLANT ☐

GROW AGAIN?   YES ☐   NO ☐

DATE	NOTES

PLANT PROFILE

COMMON NAME _____

BOTANICAL NAME _____

DATE PLANTED _____ PURCHASED AT _____

LIGHT NEEDS _____ WATER NEEDS _____

SEED ☐   TRANSPLANT ☐

GROW AGAIN?   YES ☐   NO ☐

DATE	NOTES

PLANT PROFILE

COMMON NAME _____

BOTANICAL NAME _____

DATE PLANTED _____ PURCHASED AT _____

LIGHT NEEDS _____ WATER NEEDS _____

SEED ☐   TRANSPLANT ☐

GROW AGAIN?   YES ☐   NO ☐

DATE	NOTES

PLANT PROFILE

COMMON NAME _____

BOTANICAL NAME _____

DATE PLANTED _____ PURCHASED AT _____

LIGHT NEEDS _____ WATER NEEDS _____

SEED ☐   TRANSPLANT ☐

GROW AGAIN?   YES ☐   NO ☐

DATE	NOTES

PLANT PROFILE

COMMON NAME _____

BOTANICAL NAME _____

DATE PLANTED _____ PURCHASED AT _____

LIGHT NEEDS _____ WATER NEEDS _____

SEED ☐   TRANSPLANT ☐

GROW AGAIN?   YES ☐   NO ☐

DATE	NOTES

PLANT PROFILE

COMMON NAME _____

BOTANICAL NAME _____

DATE PLANTED _____ PURCHASED AT _____

LIGHT NEEDS _____ WATER NEEDS _____

SEED ☐   TRANSPLANT ☐

GROW AGAIN?   YES ☐   NO ☐

DATE	NOTES

PLANT PROFILE

COMMON NAME _____

BOTANICAL NAME _____

DATE PLANTED _____ PURCHASED AT _____

LIGHT NEEDS _____ WATER NEEDS _____

SEED ☐   TRANSPLANT ☐

GROW AGAIN?   YES ☐   NO ☐

DATE	NOTES

PLANT PROFILE

COMMON NAME _____

BOTANICAL NAME _____

DATE PLANTED _____ PURCHASED AT _____

LIGHT NEEDS _____ WATER NEEDS _____

SEED ☐   TRANSPLANT ☐

GROW AGAIN?   YES ☐   NO ☐

DATE	NOTES

PLANT PROFILE

COMMON NAME _____

BOTANICAL NAME _____

DATE PLANTED _____ PURCHASED AT _____

LIGHT NEEDS _____ WATER NEEDS _____

SEED ☐   TRANSPLANT ☐

GROW AGAIN?   YES ☐   NO ☐

DATE	NOTES

PLANT PROFILE

COMMON NAME _____

BOTANICAL NAME _____

DATE PLANTED _____ PURCHASED AT _____

LIGHT NEEDS _____ WATER NEEDS _____

SEED ☐   TRANSPLANT ☐

GROW AGAIN?   YES ☐   NO ☐

DATE	NOTES

PLANT PROFILE

COMMON NAME _____

BOTANICAL NAME _____

DATE PLANTED _____ PURCHASED AT _____

LIGHT NEEDS _____ WATER NEEDS _____

SEED ☐   TRANSPLANT ☐

GROW AGAIN?   YES ☐   NO ☐

DATE	NOTES

PLANT PROFILE

COMMON NAME _____

BOTANICAL NAME _____

DATE PLANTED _____ PURCHASED AT _____

LIGHT NEEDS _____ WATER NEEDS _____

SEED ☐   TRANSPLANT ☐

GROW AGAIN?   YES ☐   NO ☐

DATE	NOTES

PLANT PROFILE

COMMON NAME _____

BOTANICAL NAME _____

DATE PLANTED _____ PURCHASED AT _____

LIGHT NEEDS _____ WATER NEEDS _____

SEED ☐   TRANSPLANT ☐

GROW AGAIN?   YES ☐   NO ☐

DATE	NOTES

PLANT PROFILE

COMMON NAME _____

BOTANICAL NAME _____

DATE PLANTED _____ PURCHASED AT _____

LIGHT NEEDS _____ WATER NEEDS _____

SEED ☐   TRANSPLANT ☐

GROW AGAIN?   YES ☐   NO ☐

DATE	NOTES

PLANT PROFILE

COMMON NAME _____

BOTANICAL NAME _____

DATE PLANTED _____ PURCHASED AT _____

LIGHT NEEDS _____ WATER NEEDS _____

SEED ☐   TRANSPLANT ☐

GROW AGAIN?   YES ☐   NO ☐

DATE	NOTES

PLANT PROFILE

COMMON NAME _____

BOTANICAL NAME _____

DATE PLANTED _____ PURCHASED AT _____

LIGHT NEEDS _____ WATER NEEDS _____

SEED ☐   TRANSPLANT ☐

GROW AGAIN?   YES ☐   NO ☐

DATE	NOTES

PLANT PROFILE

COMMON NAME _____

BOTANICAL NAME _____

DATE PLANTED _____ PURCHASED AT _____

LIGHT NEEDS _____ WATER NEEDS _____

SEED ☐   TRANSPLANT ☐

GROW AGAIN?   YES ☐   NO ☐

DATE	NOTES

PLANT PROFILE

COMMON NAME _____

BOTANICAL NAME _____

DATE PLANTED _____ PURCHASED AT _____

LIGHT NEEDS _____ WATER NEEDS _____

SEED ☐   TRANSPLANT ☐

GROW AGAIN?   YES ☐   NO ☐

DATE	NOTES

PLANT PROFILE

COMMON NAME _____

BOTANICAL NAME _____

DATE PLANTED _____ PURCHASED AT _____

LIGHT NEEDS _____ WATER NEEDS _____

SEED ☐   TRANSPLANT ☐

GROW AGAIN?   YES ☐   NO ☐

DATE	NOTES

PLANT PROFILE

COMMON NAME _____

BOTANICAL NAME _____

DATE PLANTED _____ PURCHASED AT _____

LIGHT NEEDS _____ WATER NEEDS _____

SEED ☐   TRANSPLANT ☐

GROW AGAIN?   YES ☐   NO ☐

DATE	NOTES

PLANT PROFILE

COMMON NAME _____

BOTANICAL NAME _____

DATE PLANTED _____ PURCHASED AT _____

LIGHT NEEDS _____ WATER NEEDS _____

SEED ☐   TRANSPLANT ☐

GROW AGAIN?   YES ☐   NO ☐

DATE	NOTES

PLANT PROFILE

COMMON NAME _____

BOTANICAL NAME _____

DATE PLANTED _____ PURCHASED AT _____

LIGHT NEEDS _____ WATER NEEDS _____

SEED ☐   TRANSPLANT ☐

GROW AGAIN?   YES ☐   NO ☐

DATE	NOTES

PLANT PROFILE

COMMON NAME _____

BOTANICAL NAME _____

DATE PLANTED _____ PURCHASED AT _____

LIGHT NEEDS _____ WATER NEEDS _____

SEED ☐   TRANSPLANT ☐

GROW AGAIN?   YES ☐   NO ☐

DATE	NOTES

PLANT PROFILE

COMMON NAME _____

BOTANICAL NAME _____

DATE PLANTED _____ PURCHASED AT _____

LIGHT NEEDS _____ WATER NEEDS _____

SEED ☐   TRANSPLANT ☐

GROW AGAIN?   YES ☐   NO ☐

DATE	NOTES

PLANT PROFILE

COMMON NAME _____

BOTANICAL NAME _____

DATE PLANTED _____ PURCHASED AT _____

LIGHT NEEDS _____ WATER NEEDS _____

SEED ☐   TRANSPLANT ☐

GROW AGAIN?   YES ☐   NO ☐

DATE	NOTES

PLANT PROFILE

COMMON NAME _____

BOTANICAL NAME _____

DATE PLANTED _____ PURCHASED AT _____

LIGHT NEEDS _____ WATER NEEDS _____

SEED ☐   TRANSPLANT ☐

GROW AGAIN?   YES ☐   NO ☐

DATE	NOTES

USE THE FOLLOWING PAGES TO PLAN
YOUR NEXT GROWING SEASON. A WISH LIST
FOR DREAMING OF THE FOLLOWING YEAR,
YEAR END NOTES ON WHAT WENT WELL
AND WHAT TO CHANGE AS WELL AS
A SUPPLIER LIST SO YOU KNOW WHERE TO
PURCHASE YOUR FAVORITES AGAIN.

THIS IS THE PERFECT TIME TO REFLECT ON THE GROWING SEASON

NEXT YEAR'S WISH LIST

ITEM

NEXT YEAR'S WISH LIST

ITEM

NEXT YEAR'S WISH LIST

ITEM

NEXT YEAR'S WISH LIST

ITEM

YEAR END NOTES.....

WHAT WENT WELL

WHAT TO CHANGE

YEAR END NOTES.....

WHAT WENT WELL

WHAT TO CHANGE

YEAR END NOTES.....

WHAT WENT WELL

_____
_____
_____
_____
_____
_____
_____
_____
_____
_____
_____
_____
_____

WHAT TO CHANGE

_____
_____
_____
_____
_____
_____
_____
_____
_____
_____
_____
_____
_____
_____

YEAR END NOTES.....

WHAT WENT WELL

_____
_____
_____
_____
_____
_____
_____
_____
_____
_____
_____
_____

WHAT TO CHANGE

_____
_____
_____
_____
_____
_____
_____
_____
_____
_____
_____
_____
_____
_____

YEAR END NOTES.....

WHAT WENT WELL

WHAT TO CHANGE

YEAR END NOTES.....

WHAT WENT WELL

___

WHAT TO CHANGE

___

SEED - PLANT - SUPPLY SOURCES

ITEM	COMPANY	PHONE	WEBSITE

SEED - PLANT - SUPPLY SOURCES

ITEM	COMPANY	PHONE	WEBSITE

SEED - PLANT - SUPPLY SOURCES

ITEM	COMPANY	PHONE	WEBSITE

SEED - PLANT - SUPPLY SOURCES

ITEM	COMPANY	PHONE	WEBSITE

Made in the USA
Las Vegas, NV
21 November 2021